The Year of the Poet VIII

May 2021

The Poetry Posse

inner child press, ltd.

The Poetry Posse 2021

Gail Weston Shazor
Shareef Abdur Rasheed
Teresa E. Gallion
hülya n. yılmaz
Kimberly Burnham
Tzemin Ition Tsai
Elizabeth Esguerra Castillo
Jackie Davis Allen
Joe Paire
Caroline 'Ceri' Nazareno
Ashok K. Bhargava
Alicja Maria Kuberska
Swapna Behera
Albert 'Infinite' Carrasco
Eliza Segiet
William S. Peters, Sr.

~ * ~

In order to maintain each poet's authentic voice, this volume has not undergone the scrutiny of editing. Please take time to indulge each contributor for their own creativity and aspirations to convey their uniqueness.

hülya n. yılmaz, Ph.D.
Director of Editing ~
Inner Child Press International

General Information

The Year of the Poet VIII
May 2021 Edition

The Poetry Posse

1st Edition : 2021

This Publishing is protected under Copyright Law as a "Collection". All rights for all submissions are retained by the Individual Author and or Artist. No part of this Publishing may be Reproduced, Transferred in any manner without the prior **WRITTEN CONSENT** of the "Material Owners" or its Representative Inner Child Press. Any such violation infringes upon the Creative and Intellectual Property of the Owner pursuant to International and Federal Copyright Laws. Any queries pertaining to this "Collection" should be addressed to Publisher of Record.

Publisher Information
1st Edition : Inner Child Press
intouch@innerchildpress.com
www.innerchildpress.com

This Collection is protected under U.S. and International Copyright Laws

Copyright © 2021 : The Poetry Posse

ISBN-13 : 978-1-952081-49-1 (inner child press, ltd.)

$ 12.99

WHAT WOULD LIFE BE WITHOUT A LITTLE POETRY?

Dedication

This Book is dedicated to

Humanity, Peace & Poetry

the Power of the Pen

can effectuate change!

&

The Poetry Posse

past, present & future

our Patrons and Readers

the Spirit of our Everlasting Muse

*In the darkness of my life
I heard the music
I danced...
and the Light appeared
and I dance*

Janet P. Caldwell

Table of Contents

Foreword .... *ix*
Preface .... *xiii*
The Feature Diego Rivera .... *xv*

The Poetry Posse

Gail Weston Shazor 1
Alicja Maria Kuberska 7
Jackie Davis Allen 13
Tezmin Ition Tsai 19
Shareef Abdur – Rasheed 25
Kimberly Burnham 33
Elizabeth Esguerra Castillo 39
Joe Paire 45
hülya n. yılmaz 51
Teresa E. Gallion 57
Ashok K. Bhargava 63
Caroline Nazareno-Gabis 69

Table of Contents ... *continued*

Swapna Behera	75
Albert Carassco	81
Eliza Segiet	87
William S. Peters, Sr.	93

May's Featured Poets — 101

Paramita Mukherjee Mullick	103
Jaydeep Sarangi	109
Rose Zerguine	115
Bismay Mohanty	123

Inner Child News — 133
Other Anthological Works — 165

Foreword

The month of May this year marks for the book in your hands a commemoration of an art piece by Diego Rivera. "I paint what I see" is a statement attributed to this phenomenal visual artist. The context from which this assertion originates concerns artistic integrity as Rivera had viewed it. In our interpretations of the focal mural, we had no other option but to compose poems that depend on how we (want to) see his creative work. Had he lived today, would he have approved our varying observations of the one and the same fresco? Most probably, yes. For this monthly publication's contributors have, as in all past times, embraced the principle of "integrity" with high respect. While none of us could answer the rhetorical question above, each of us have committed ourselves into doing extensive research on the life and work of this prominent Mexican painter.

The field of art historiography recognizes Diego Rivera as a revolutionary painter. His frescoes have been and continue to be celebrated as the birth of a mural movement in Mexican and international art. Having started his art studies at the age of ten, a multitude of opportunities accompanied Rivera. His 15-year long stay in Europe – primarily in Paris, a prevalent destination point for young European and American artists and writers, exposed him to various art movements, including Cubism which Pablo Picasso was leading. After he welcomed the realistic and post-impressionistic art styles, his paintings began to attract a growing attention outside Paris. His preference during that time to use simple forms and large areas of vibrant colors had made a significant impact in- as well as outside widely noted art circles. Following his life in Europe, Rivera painted murals throughout Mexico and in a considerable part of the US. Thanks to his extensive and innovative work between 1922 and 1953, the concept of public art was rediscovered.

The reinvented public art which materialized in the hands of Diego Rivera in the 20th century is here to guide us in our era along the poems composed in his art's honor. As we approach one mural by this ground breaking painter, we would like to invite you to hold dear the story behind it. Not unlike his other paintings, Rivera has engraved a story also on this fresco, a story reflective of his life and work at large. His own words in *My Art, My Life* attest to this fact:

> As an artist, I have always tried to be faithful to my vision of life, and I have frequently been in conflict with those who wanted me to paint not what I saw but what they wished me to see.

We hope that you will enjoy today's poetic journey on the international platform of *The Year of the Poet* through this artist's mural of our designation. In our creative treatment of the selected painting, we have "tried to be faithful" to the painter's "vision of life" as reflected in the quote above. May we not belong among those people with whom Diego Rivera was in conflict when his view of his own art was concerned.

hülya n. yılmaz [sic]

Professor Emerita (Liberal Arts, Penn State, USA)
Director of Editing Services at Inner Child Press (USA)
Published tri-lingual author
Literary translator

Poets, Writers . . . know that we are the enchanting magicians that nourishes the seeds of dreams and thoughts . . . it is our words that entice the hearts and minds of others to believe there is something grand about the possibilities that life has to offer and our words tease it forth into action . . . for you are the Poet, the Writer to whom the Gift of Words has been entrusted . . .

~ wsp

Preface

Dear Family and Friends,

So, here we are, beginning our eighth year of monthly publication of *The Year of the Poet*. Amazing how much effort has been given by all the poets, to include the various members of *The Poetry Posse* and all the wonderful featured poets from all over our world. For myself, it has been and continues to be a great honor to be a part of this wonderful cooperative effort.

Last year, 2020 has been challenging for many of us throughout the year. We at *Inner Child Press International* were busy. We envisioned our role where the arts meet humanity to continue doing what we were good at . . . publishing. We managed to not only produce and publish this series, *The Year of the Poet* each month, but we were also very proactive in the arena of human and social consciousness. We were able to produce several other anthologies to include: World Healing, World Peace 2020; CORONA . . . social distancing; The Heart of a Poet; W.A.R. . . we are revolution; Poetry, the Best of 2020. Going forward, we are seeking to invest in the same or greater effort towards contributing to a 'conscious humanity'. We, poets and writers do have something to say about it all, and we intend to do so in any and every way we can. So stay tuned . . .

Bill

William S. Peters, Sr.

Publisher
Inner Child Press International

www.innerchildpress.com

PS

Do Not forget about the World Healing, World Peace Poetry initiative for 2022. Mark your calendars. Submissions will be opening . . .
September 1st 2021

Past volumes are vailable here

www.worldhealingworldpeacepoetry.com

For Free Downloads of Previous Issues of The Year of the Poet

www.innerchildpress.com/the-year-of-the-poet

Diego Rivera

May 2021

In 1922, Diego Rivera started a series of 124 frescoes for the Secretariat of Public Education in Mexico City. It took him six years to complete the project. A founding member of the Revolutionary Union of Technical Workers, Painters and Sculptors, Diego Rivera's art dealt with Mexican society and Mexico's 1910 Revolution. Rivera developed his own style based on large, simplified figures and bold colors with an Aztec influence.

"As an artist I have always tried to be faithful to my vision of life, and I have frequently been in conflict with those who wanted me to paint not what I saw

but what they wished me to see." ~Diego Rivera, My Art, My Life

https://www.wikigallery.org/paintings/295001-295500/295345/painting1.jpg

https://upload.wikimedia.org/wikipedia/commons/thumb/5/58/Diego_Rivera's_Mural_in_Acapulco%2C_Mexico.jpg/1280px-Diego_Rivera's_Mural_in_Acapulco%2C_Mexico.jpg

*Poets . . .
sowing seeds in the
Conscious Garden of Life,
that those who have yet to come
may enjoy the Flowers.*

Poetry succeeds where instruction fails.

~ wsp

Gail Weston Shazor

Gail Weston Shazor

This is a creative promise ~ my pen will speak to and for the world. Enamored with letters and respectful of their power, I have been writing for most of my life. A mother, daughter, sister and grandmother I give what I have been given, greatfilledly.

Author of . . .

"An Overstanding of an Imperfect Love"
&
Notes from the Blue Roof

Lies My Grandfathers Told Me

available at Inner Child Press.

www.facebook.com/gailwestonshazor
www.innerchildpress.com/gail-weston-shazor
navypoet1@gmail.com

Diego, my dear Diego

You visioned the revolution
In artful brushstrokes
Pulling the pigment of pain
From peasants
Grains groaning against
A free sky
Greens and oranges and wheat
Grown not for the masses
But the masters
Acoustically driven by lyrics
In burnt yellows
Diego, Frida's Diego
With a lust for everything
And everyone
We know the story
Immortalized on film
Committed to memories
And even in death
You are one with the call to equality

A Senryu
A Haiku
A Nonet
A Couplet
And a dream
Greying dreams transmute
Old memories into dust
Across still water
Drums always will beat
Requiring attention
Of a calling sound
The
Movement
Make cadence
Of the notes
Gathered on the wind
The breath of whispering
And the black soil of the earth
The offering of new rainfalls
Until it is now in completion
I threw the jagged edges of the broken pieces
Into the rising sun

At the Crossroads
Palindrome

Heart wynd crossroads
Tall grows the wall
Voice and mind says
Yet and
Knows no edges
Misunderstanding not
Kisses stolen
Skin to skin want
Light of dawn
SLEEPING
Dawn of light
Want skin to skin
Stolen kisses
Not misunderstanding
Edges no knows
And yet
Says mind and voice
And the wall grows tall
Crossroads wynd heart

Alicja Maria Kuberska

Alicja Maria Kuberska

Alicja Maria Kuberska – awarded Polish poetess, novelist, journalist, editor.

She is a member of the Polish Writers Associations in Warsaw, Poland and IWA Bogdani, Albania. She is also a member of directors' board of Soflay Literature Foundation, Our Poetry Archive (India) and Cultural Ambassador for Poland (Inner Child Press, USA)

Her poems have been published in numerous anthologies and magazines in : Poland, Czech Republic, Slovakia, Hungary,Ukraina, Belgium, Bulgaria, Albania, Spain, the UK, Italy, the USA, Canada, the UK, Argentina, Chile, Peru, Israel, Turkey, India, Uzbekistan, South Korea, Taiwan, China, Australia, South Africa, Zambia, Nigeria

She received two medals - the Nosside UNESCO Competition in Italy (2015) and European Academy of Science Arts and Letters in France (2017). Ahe also received a reward of international literary competition in Italy „ Tra le parole e 'elfinito" (2018). She was announced a poet of the 2017 year by Soflay Literature Foundation (2018).She also received : Bolesław Prus Prize Poland (2019), Culture Animator Poland (2019) and first prize Premio Internazionale di Poesia Poseidonia- Paestrum Italy (2019).

My art is my life
For Diego Rivera

Everyone has a different vision of life.

He saw things
which people could not see
- other colors and shapes
emerged from his imagination,
Aztec patterns returned
and dream figures appeared.
Color took on boldness
to spread out like a bright glow
on a blue background.

Being an artist means
that you should be true to yourself
and paint what you see,
not what the public wants to see.

The world is a great illusion.

The matches

I am a child
that has not been blessed.
I stand at a street corner
with matches in my hands
and light my dreams with little sparks.

I know why it is so
and understand what happened.
My clock did not strike happy hours…
Or maybe didn't strike them
often enough

A stranger

It seems to me,
I know her from somewhere.
The familiar eyes look at me.
A smile lights up her face.

She holds a diploma in hand
And believes that she can easily
Change a man and the world.
Naive girl.

Young mother
Matured with love.
Secrets of the night were to be
The happiness of days.

Power suited business woman
Sells her soul for pennies
And is screwed by corporations.
One day she will wake up.

Time is merciful
It steals moments from memory
Leaving only small fragments
And whispers of her behind

Jackie Davis Allen

Jackie Davis Allen

Jackie Davis Allen, otherwise known as Jacqueline D. Allen or Jackie Allen, grew up in the Cumberland Mountains of Appalachia. As the next eldest daughter of a coal miner father and a stay at home mother, she was the first in her family to attend and graduate from college. Her siblings, in their own right, are accomplished, though she is the only one, to date, that has discovered the gift of writing.

Graduating from Radford University, with a Bachelors of Science degree in Early Education, she taught in both public and private schools. For over a decade she taught private art classes to children both in her home and at a local Art and Framing Shop where she also sold her original soft sculptured Victorian dolls and original christening gowns.

She resides in northern Virginia with her husband, taking much needed get-aways to their mountain home near the Blue Ridge Mountains, a place that evokes memories of days spent growing up in the Appalachian Mountains.

A lover of hats, she has worn many. Following marriage to her college sweetheart, and as wife, mother, grandmother, teacher, tutor, artist, writer, poet and crafter, she is a lover of art and antiques, surrounding herself, always, with books, seeking to learn more.

In 2015 she authored *Looking for Rainbows, Poetry, Prose and Art*, and in 2017, *Dark Side of the Moon*. Both books of mostly narrative poetry were published by Inner Child Press and were edited by hulya n. yilmaz.

in 2019, No Illusions.Through the Looking Glass, which was nominated to be considered for a Pulitzer Prize by the publisher and editor of InnerChild Press, ltd.

http://www.innerchildpress.com/jackie-davis-allen.php
jackiedavisallen.com

caution

behind
mind's eye
a caution exists

on screen
of introspection
blinks boldly, a light

there, wherein, exists
a cautionary white light
of reality's vision

breathe

breathe,
acknowledge life;
live life passionately,
exuberantly

see the flowers
in all of their beauty,
the flowers
are perfuming the air

branches of grace
are reaching out;
be one, welcome
one and all

like songbirds,
let us embrace life, love;
despite different songs,
no matter the tune

be happy,
sing songs of joy
breathe in the moment
live in the moment

Jackie Davis Allen

Blue

Blue against blue,
The lofty ridge tops kiss the sky.
Fluffy white clouds descend,

Into the equalizing fog.

Obscured, the mountains
Yet still beautiful,
Once sun bestows its revealing rays.

Time immortal, always there,
These mountains, I've come to know.
Beloved, discovered

By natives and nature.

Each echoes the refrain
Of God's wonderful creation.
Renewed by seasons' change,

Ancient and mountainous,
They rise up ever so high.
Still they are same. Yet different.

Intimate memories linger;

Enhancing views remain,
Whether from Trillium fields
Or awesome overlooks.

Tzemin Ition Tsai

Dr. Tzemin Ition Tsai (蔡澤民博士) was born in Republic of China, in 1957. He holds a Ph.D. in Chemical Engineering and two Masters of Science in Applied Mathematics and Chemical Engineering. He is a professor at Asia University (Taiwan), editor of "Reading, Writing and Teaching" academic text. He also writes the long-term columns for Chinese Language Monthly in Taiwan.

He is a scholar with a wide range of expertise, while maintaining a common and positive interest in science, engineering and literature member. He is also an editor of "Reading, Writing and Teaching" academic text and a columnist for *'Chinese Language Monthly'* in Taiwan

He has won many national literary awards. His literary works have been anthologized and published in books, journals, and newspapers in more than 40 countries and have been translated into more than a dozen languages.

Mural Story

Sunday afternoon
It's as sunny as an atheist's dream
God no longer wants to exist in simple forms and simple
　　forms and large patches of vivid colors
However, that Post-Impressionism can't get rid of
Cannibal activities in the so-called
The taste of the brain brought all the listener were deeply
　　moved
No one minds
This suspicious claim under a well-planned lie
When man evolves a civilization higher than the
　　mechanized
But still primitive one he has now
For then
Man will have thrown off all of his superstitions and
　　irrational taboos

Murals
Only painted on the high wall at the end of the street
Tells the story of inner silence
Tierra Fecundada
Fertile Land depicts
The revolutionary struggles of Mexico's peasant and
　　working classes
Hammer and sickle
That woman with an ear of corn
In the corn field, bodies lie down and fertilize
A sunflower
Glorifies those who died for an ideal
And are reborn, transfigured, into the fertile cornfield of the
　　nation

Jade Butterfly

Pieces of water be cut in the air, cleverly dressed up the
 winter scenery, illuminating the lake
Gradually the flower balls turn into catkins, and the elm
 pods fly around
Scattered silver wine glasses, chasing horses from time to
 time
White ribbons are tight, fluttering with the carriages one by
 one
All over the curtain corner
Icy bamboo chopsticks grow out in the cold, like pearls
 under light dissection

Should we drink a sip of wine and sing softly?
The felt hanging around the red tent which adorns the
 golden furnace allows for ancestor worship like a wild
 beast
Turning to face the tall building, drunkenly chanting that
 thank-you speech for mother's birthday
Time has stopped, the sound of bamboo is like a rocky
 thick valley
Overwhelming everything, including the moving shadows
 of birds following the river
Endless hesitation lies in my heart
The singing in the distance is like an exhausted gem, so
 similar to that ode I made

Snow Remains As Tidbits

The smoke that fills the entire mountain forest
In Spring, it still doesn't want to return home
Snow flies up to the sun
In consort two or three together
Wickers, don't go against
The will of Heaven
The reflections of the embankment are blowing on the water
It seems ever more difficult to leave

Although the snow covered the mountains and plains
The tidbits are still unwilling to let go of their beauty
The giant sun has no more taboos to break
Have to enjoy together with its bustling
Born as an emperor
But in the soldiers' camp

Shareef Abdur Rasheed

Shareef Abdur Rasheed

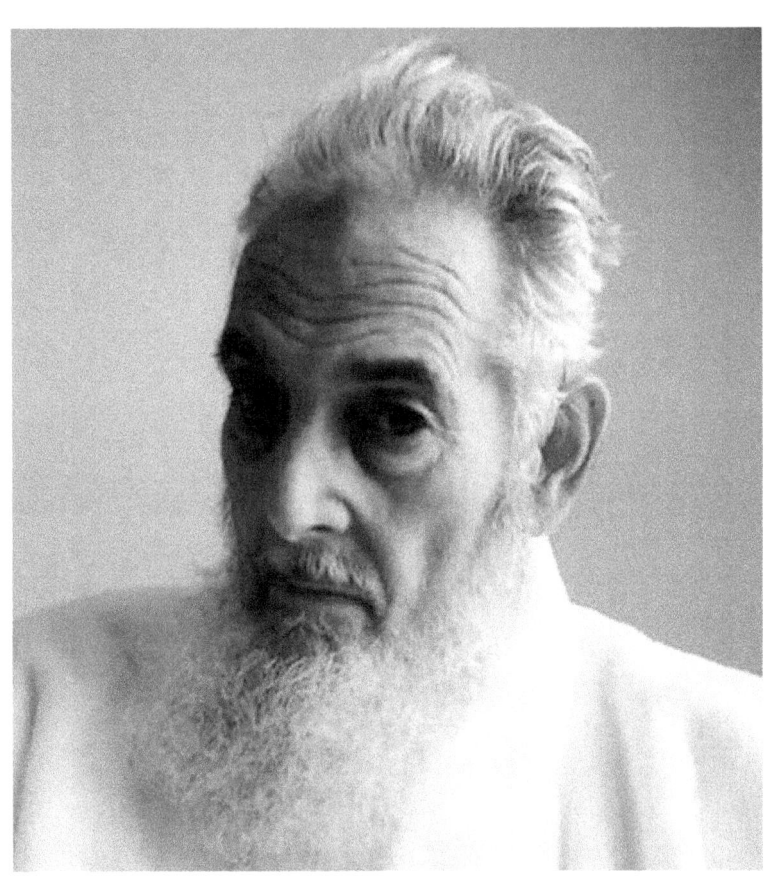

Shareef Abdur-Rasheed, AKA Zakir Flo was born and raised in Brooklyn, New York. His education includes Brooklyn College, Suffolk County Community College and Makkah, Saudi Arabia. He is a Veteran of the Viet Nam era, where in 1969 he reverted to his now reverently embraced Islamic Faith. He is very active in the Islamic community and beyond with his teachings, activism and his humanity.

Shareef's spiritual expression comes through the persona of "Zakir Flo". Zakir is Arabic for "To remind". Never silent, Shareef Abdur-Rasheed is always dropping science, love, consciousness and signs of the time in rhyme.

Shareef is the Patriarch of the Abdur-Rasheed Family with 9 Children (6 Sons and 3 Daughters) and 41 Grandchildren (24 Boys and 17 Girls).

For more information about Shareef, visit his personal FaceBook Page at :

https://www.facebook.com/shareef.abdurrasheed1
https://zakirflo.wordpress.com

Shareef Abdur Rasheed

Diego

Renowned artist (B:1889 D:1957)
born: Mexico
artistic talent appeared early
groomed, trained, traveled
Madrid, Paris development
metamorphosis
traveled through phases
constitute layers humans indulgments
certainly, socio-political realities
captured Diego's expression
after going through phases of
artistic travel settled on humanity
good, bad, ugly, beauty in diversity
Diego expressed these in his themes
depiction, people toiling in the fields
gathering harvest
people backbone of industrial growth
their struggles, celebrations of life
familia! heart of humanity
expressed through strokes
dispel yokes of dismissal
indifference, ignorance, elitist leanings
classes, clashing, well-endowed abundance
vs depravation, curse of lands
tribes, nations
Marxist adherence even Leon Trotsky and
wife in exile lived with Rivera, Mexico City
himself, comrades like Che Guevara stood
out as symbols of rage against corrupted,
nations engaged in persecution, exploitation
it's peoples denied self-expression, free thought

Rivera's work included shining light on western
industrialization on backs of the people thee
essential backbone inspiration FDR's
WPA program
world renown muralist, example
consisting of 27 panels
Detroit Industry murals depict ascent
Ford Motor Company featuring working
class men and women
social/political makeup
Mexico the people,
from elite wealthy to working class
Dream of a Sunday Afternoon in Alameda Park
all walks but not without conflict, abuse, neglect
depiction: decorated skeleton in the middle of
very diverse cross-section
so much to cover, Diego's works his amazing
influence as an artist with profound conscious
speaking through his art addressing the human
story, good, bad, ugly

Shareef Abdur Rasheed

Blessed be..,

the peace makers dem vibe on all humanities tribes
" *Bani Adam(aws)** " all have to answer the same call
to serve, give, help, assist, relieve, release, rescue, feed,
clothe, shelter who need love, yearn to be human
blessed be the humble slaves of the one true merciful
master, who fashioned us all said " be " and we were
and are through undeserved mercy all that are, all who
ever was received and continues to receive mercy
yet do we reflect, better yet do we respect the sanctity
of life, your own and all others who possess the same
loan?
do we know the blessings bestowed on the kind hearted?
who reach out to the displaced, fragmented, vilified,
shunned, cast away reduced to invisible, non-existent
by those blinded by the bling in the world of fake things
who they compete to be kings and queens?
love ' n ' mercy is the real thing, priceless!
though many fail to overstand, perceptions flawed
dem remain in awe of superficial, empty, void of substance
this being the glitter that blinds many amongst us
blinded by the fake light of darkness that which is a,
mirage that takes souls away
and the peace loving pray for the earth to be at peace
one day and strive while they're alive to make it that way
day by day give of that which they received as a loan
one never owed, one never owned dem gave back and
received immeasurably bounties one would find it hard
to believe that by giving you receive so that your cup
overflows as does your worth as a human being grows ' n '
grows, this the humble, compassionate, caring peace lovers
know

food4thought = education

Miraculous

miracles abound
are you looking around,
what have you found?
just take a look around
to sky, to ground
stop listen to the sound
it's life all around
what is it you're looking
for?
shiny things that go
ching a ching
or spiritual things that
sooth your very being?
remove nightmares
with sweet dreams
stop the screams
listen to birds sing
yes, life's a short fling
why you indulge in wrong
things
dem drain life from your being
nothing but strife shows up
on the screen
cut that part out of the play
replace with lines that say
"do righteousness everyday "
be patient, pray
listen to the cries of the hungry
say that could be me
feed dem plenty true
your plate will stay full

Shareef Abdur Rasheed

give and you receive
joy instead of grief
yes, listen to the sound
so that your feet stay firmly
planted on the ground

food4thought = education

Kimberly Burnham

Kimberly Burnham

A brain health expert with a PhD in Integrative Medicine, Kimberly Burnham has lived in tropical Colombia; in Belgium during the Vietnam War; in Japan teaching businessmen English; in diverse international Toronto, Canada; and several places in the US. Now, she's in Spokane, WA with her wife, Elizabeth, two sets of twins (age 11 & 14) and three dogs. Her recent book, *Awakenings: Peace Dictionary, Language and the Mind, a Daily Brain Health Program* includes the word for peace in hundreds of languages. Her poetry weaves through 80+ volumes of *The Year of the Poet*, *Inspired by Gandhi*, *Women Building the World*, and *A Woman's Place in the Dictionary*. She is currently working on several ekphrastic writing projects. One is a novel, *Art Thief Cracks Healing Code for Parkinson's Disease* and the other is non-fiction, *Using Ekphrastic Fiction Writing and Poetry to Create Interest and Promote Artists, Writers, and Poets*.

http://www.NerveWhisperer.Solutions

https://healthy-brain.medium.com/bears-at-the-window-of-climate-change-d1fb403eeaf3

Seeing Art

Each piece a vision
of the artist created
in a certain medium
paint, oil, water,
ink, ceramic, wood
on a particular surface
canvas, paper, earth
each choice influences what I see
in sweat, blood and energy
how I feel about the art
reflected in
manifested from
the life of the artist

What I See

I worry about what I see
in the faces of those around me
how I feel when I see
suffering, poverty, hunger
a need to start a revolution

Try to describe what I see
with solutions
ways I perceive
make the world better

I can't change what I see
but I can change what I do
with my vision
I can change what my children will see
in the distant future
beyond me

The Art of Each Revolution

The wheel turns
turning birth to childhood
hoody-clad teens grow
grown adults still learning
learn so much before death

Death stalking the art of each revolution
revolving around the sun the earth
on earth to learn and give birth create!
creates a better place and love
love life until joy bursts
a burst of energy turning the wheel
wheels at the heart of each evolution

Elizabeth E. Castillo

Elizabeth Esguerra Castillo

Elizabeth Esguerra Castillo is a multi-awarded and an Internationally-Published Contemporary Author/Poet and a Professional Writer / Creative Writer / Feature Writer / Journalist / Travel Writer from the Philippines. She has 2 published books, "Seasons of Emotions" (UK) and "Inner Reflections of the Muse", (USA). Elizabeth is also a co-author to more than 60 international anthologies in the USA, Canada, UK, Romania, India. She is a Contributing Editor of Inner Child Magazine, USA and an Advisory Board Member of Reflection Magazine, an international literary magazine. She is a member of the American Authors Association (AAA) and PEN International.

Web links:

Facebook Fan Page

https://free.facebook.com/ElizabethEsguerraCastillo

Google Plus

https://plus.google.com/u/0/+ElizabethCastillo

No Façade

I am more than conventional

Not to be dictated by anyone

My ideas are precious, not imitations,

If there are phantoms lurking

In a society that keeps on changing,

My art will depict what my eyes really see

I'll let the ghosts and skeletons out

No façade can block the naked truth.

Ambedo

There's something lyrical about
The way you entered my life,
Simply poetic, you are like
The mystic verses weaved by my muse
Vividly, I remember you in my dreams,
As a lonely boy by the waterfalls
Reflecting on the essence of the
Ebb and flow of life.
Innuendos-
There is Oneness in our beautiful coincidences
For long after you've crossed The Great Beyond,
Your golden heart still lingers-
Like a beautiful disaster, a dramatic tragedy,
Daydreaming amid the bareness of trees
Leaves have fallen when dawn came.
Our souls crossed paths in the innocence of youth
One summer day our Lights collided
Years passed we have gotten older
Then destiny made a way for us to meet once more,
The fondness for solitude we share
The worlds we explored only we can understand.
December dawned while you were away,
The emptiness brought me into the abyss
Searching for my Twin Flame
And one September morn, you chased the Light,
My walls collapsed, uncertainty lingered
Grief have stolen the smile on my face
Your loss catapulted me into the Ambedo.

The Supernova in the Night Sky

People come into our lives to hold up a mirror,
A reflection of who we truly are
Illuminating the beauty that already resides in us
Some can be iconic sparks of enlightenment,
To help us sing back the lost melody in our hearts
When mere words have gone mad and the rhythm drums a different beat.
There are simply those who amplify the light,
And reflect where it originated from- the Source
The angel in the night who rescues us from the darkness,
Teaching us to love ourselves once more,
And to bring out the Empathic Soul in us.
The magical moment when you open yourself up to connect the Cosmic Dots,
When the alchemical marriage of the Divine Feminine and the Sacred Masculine takes place
And this paves the way for you to embrace your Higher Self- a destined conduit to the stars,
The supernova in the night sky where you witness a crusade of fireflies with wings emitting Pure Light,
This is when the Legend of a New World takes its daring, mystic flight!

Joe Paire

Joe Paire

Joseph L Paire' aka Joe DaVerbal Minddancer . . . is a quiet man, born in a time where civil liberties were a walk on thin ice. He's been a victim of his own shyness often sidelined in his own quest for love. He became the observer, charting life's path. Taking note of the why, people do what they do. His writings oft times strike a cord with the dormant strings of the reader. His pen the rosined bow drawn across the mind. He comes full-frontal or in the subtlest way, always expressing in a way that stimulate the senses.

www.facebook.com/joe.minddancer

It's A Diego Rivera

What a day for a stroll.
I'd love to show you off to the world.
Look at us with neighbors and family.
Jealousy seen through lips that curl.

It's a day for festivities and you're a shy one.
There are lovely balloons I think I'll buy one.
let bygones be bygones,
let's not take notice of the frowns.

Here come the clowns and hoopla
Carnival people who'll dupe y'all
The colors of life are in bloom.
The intricacies of a mural drawn to mirror you.

Can't you see you're beautiful,
Why don't you smile, while fruitful!
I'm just thrilled to be with such company.
I think it may rain today!

I think I may paint today, green and yellow leaves.
Purple stoic trees, they way you stand by me.
the way an artist sees the world.
Rose colored lens can never match the soul's eye.

Sell It Off

How often have I sold a precious memento?
Years of collections given up for the taxman.
One airplane could cost billions, but we front the debt.

One plane could explain the disparity gained.
They take from Peter to pay Paul.
The effects from either and they'll fall.

Sell the years of tears shed, all that metal and all.
You're meddling with all who sacrificed for the call.
Public school funding, housing for the homeless.

Why do we need new tanks?
We have enough for war times three.
How about a little medicine for free?

How many remember no lock on your door.
If you starve the people, you rob the people.
None of whom truly voted for war.

Sell it off, those war machines.
Sell it off so this debt will be clean.
Your credit score is running mean.

Sell the war back, those antique rifles.
Invest in the populous, you know the lives that matter.
Shattered dreams over war machines.

Take stock in the people you've used as stock!
Look back at the aftermath of wars inherent evil.
Sell back the pain, know what I mean.

Joe Paire

A Day In Spring

I talked with love today.
I didn't talk by speaking, I thought by thinking.
It's a beautiful day, no matter what I'd say.
It's a beautiful day and rain is in the forecast.

Rains become at long last, nothing to fear.
Speak when spoken too, leaves feelings of solitude.
I'll greet the bee when all I see is honey.
I'll flee the sting and laughter during my scurry.

Pavement cracks hold life so dear.
They hold an image, but I don't have my camera.
I don't have the grammar sometimes to express my view.
Every passing minute, there's a growth spurt.

And this squirrel has no idea what I'm saying.
What I'm saying is that spring is a living thing.
Much like winter who's trembled lips just because.
You'll wear a sweater well, just because.

But spring in its own raison d'être
Gives me reason to speak to its leaves.
I've tasted its breeze though some may sneeze.
I told her; I'll be back tomorrow with a snapshot in voice.

hülya n. yılmaz

hülya n. yılmaz

Professor Emerita (Humanities, Penn State, USA), hülya n. yılmaz [sic] is a published tri-lingual author, literary translator, and Director of Editing Services (Inner Child Press International, USA). Her work has appeared in numerous anthologies of global endeavors and was presented at poetry events in the U.S. and abroad. In 2018, the WIN of British Colombia, Canada honored yılmaz with a literary excellence award. Her two poems remain permanently installed in *Telepoem Booth* (USA). hülya finds it vital for everyone to understand a deeper sense of self, and writes creatively to attain a comprehensive awareness for and development of our humanity.

Writing Web Site
https://hulyanyilmaz.com/

Editing Web Site
https://hulyasfreelancing.com

"God is dead"

when Nietzsche revealed the motives rooted in
traditional Western religion, morality, and philosophy
in the 19th century,
he secured himself a timeless prominence
as one of Europe's most influential intellectuals

the secularism of the Enlightenment era
is said to have enabled
this half-blind, seriously ill and pained thinker
his famed enquiry during his late years
his scrutiny of the concept of God, that is

in his latest masterpieces,
among which *The Antichrist* stands out,
the philosopher attacks the "slave morality"
of Western Christianity and its "apathy"

Nietzsche's objection to institutionalized religions
marks his journey into an interrogation of the forbidden

with his invitation to his readers
to contemplate on the death of God,
to imagine the experience of despair over that death,
thus, to give a chance to a new meaning of life . . .
this 19th century philosopher seems to have reached
beyond the boundaries of the country of his birth

could Diego Rivera have possibly been influenced
by his contemporaneous counterpart
in the making of his mural
Dreams of a Sunday in the Alameda?

"God does not exist"

picture an eminent mural by Diego Rivera, please
Dreams of a Sunday in the Alameda, for instance,
with a sign in the hands of Don Ignacio Ramírez:
"God does not exist"

a public furor ensues
the artist is asked to remove the inscription
he refuses to abide by such demands

the painting goes into a 9-year-long prison
Rivera finally agrees to eliminate
the controversial phrase
but first, he avows his atheist stance
and attests his views on religions:
"a form of collective neurosis"

art and its viewers

artistic integrity in painting . . .
as in, "I paint what I see",
per Rivera's own words

gets violated as a creative presentation

as long as we, the observers,
see not what an artist sees
but rather what we want them to see

in sum: what we see

Teresa
E.
Gallion

Teresa E. Gallion

Teresa E. Gallion was born in Shreveport, Louisiana and moved to Illinois at the age of 15. She completed her undergraduate training at the University of Illinois Chicago and received her master's degree in Psychology from Bowling Green State University in Ohio. She retired from New Mexico state government in 2012.

She moved to New Mexico in 1987. While writing sporadically for many years, in 1998 she started reading her work in the local Albuquerque poetry community. She has been a featured reader at local coffee houses, bookstores, art galleries, museums, libraries, Outpost Performance Space, the Route 66 Festival in 2001 and the State of Oklahoma's Poetry Festival in Cheyenne, Oklahoma in 2004. She occasionally hosts an open mic.

Teresa's work is published in numerous Journals and anthologies. She has two CDs: *On the Wings of the Wind* and *Poems from Chasing Light*. She has published three books: *Walking Sacred Ground, Contemplation in the High Desert* and *Chasing Light*.

Chasing Light was a finalist in the 2013 New Mexico/Arizona Book Awards.

The surreal high desert landscape and her personal spiritual journey influence the writing of this Albuquerque poet. When she is not writing, she is committed to hiking the enchanted landscapes of New Mexico. You may preview her work at

http://bit.ly/1aIVPNq or *http://bit.ly/13IMLGh*

Dark Chaos

The dark shadows of his soul
follow him into the circus
of his ego.

Finely dressed, he stands
in front of the crowd
as if he is important.

His darkness dressed in white
is a skeleton that
overshadows his joy.

His unhappiness is hard
to hide when you look
deeply into his shocked eyes.

Leak in Feelings

The eruption of time
bleeds on the sidewalk.
You beat a rigid heart
back into its cave.
Fear of being hurt
is a slow walk
to the dust you will become.

The geese do an air ritual
across an exotic blue blanket.
The pigeon that adores you
paces on the mesa
holding tight to hope,
squeezing the juice of denial,
licking it off your bones.

You feel nothing in the moment,
but healing is coming.
The black theater of night
sweats with the moisture of pain released,
opens the possibility for love
to enter your scarred domain.

Catch Up

My blood has traveled
four thousand years
across many lifetimes
to get to this tree
that knows my true heart.

I walk boldly into its branches,
hug the trunk as if we were
old lovers meeting after
a thousand years break.

I can hear the whispers
in my head, hello friend,
so nice to feel your presence.
It has been a rough four thousand.
I missed your loving hugs.
Sit next to me. Let's talk.
We have a lot of catch up to do.

Ashok K. Bhargava

Ashok K. Bhargava

Ashok Bhargava is a poet, writer, community activist, public speaker, management consultant and a keen photographer. Based in Vancouver, he has published several collections of his poems: Riding the Tide, Mirror of Dreams, A Kernel of Truth, Skipping Stones, Half Open Door and Lost in the Morning Calm. His poetry has been published in various literary magazines and anthologies.

Ashok is a Poet Laureate and poet ambassador to Japan, Korea and India. He is founder of WIN: Writers International Network Canada. Its main objective is to inspire, encourage, promote and recognize writers of diverse genres, artists and community leaders. He has received many accolades including Nehru Humanitarian Award for his leadership of Writers International Network Canada, Poets without Borders Peace Award for his journeys across the globe to celebrate peace and to create alliances with poets, and Kalidasa Award for creative writings.

To Diego Rivera

I wander around
With earth beneath my feet and
Sky in my hands.

I want to touch your paintings
Blooming with folks and machines
Showering petals from the ceiling.

My novice heart afraid not to
Offend archangels
By praising your works.

I immerse myself
In your paints
To become you, your painting.

Don't Regret and Don't Forget

Today is a colorful day,
blossoms bend like an arch
in the perfumed fresh wind.

Silky sun-rays are warm,
the birds fly around
with melodies of delight.

I step into crystal clear water
that has absorbed
ashes and bones of my ancestors.

It makes me realize
that I will reap eternity here
when it will absorb my ashes too.

I see distant things
as if they were close and
take a distanced view of close things.

Truth must be seen as
what it is,
not what I want it to be.

Fluid Poetry

Poetry can be
shaped,
curved,
bent and
formed
to flow
freely.

A poet can
differ,
disrupt and
break from
paradigms
written
before him
to show
his / her
individuality,
originality and
creativity
better than
a cookie cutter.

Caroline 'Ceri Naz' Nazareno Gabis

Carolin 'Ceri' Nazareno-Gabis

Caroline 'Ceri Naz' Nazareno-Gabis, author of Velvet Passions of Calibrated Quarks, World Poetry Canada International Director to Philippines is known as a 'poet of peace and friendship', a multi-awarded poet, editor, journalist, speaker, linguist, educator, peace and women's advocate. She believes that learning other's language and culture is a doorway to wisdom.

Among her poetic belts include PANORAMA YOUTH LITERARY AWARDS 2020, 7 th Prize Winner in the 19th, 20th and 21st Italian Award of Literary Festival; Writers International Network-Canada ''Amazing Poet 2015'', The Frang Bardhi Literary Prize 2014 (Albania), the sair-gazeteci or Poet Journalist Award 2014 (Tuzla, Istanbul, Turkey) and World Poetry Empowered Poet 2013 (Vancouver, Canada). She's a featured member of Association of Women's Rights and Development (AWID), The Poetry Posse, Galaktika Poetike, Asia Pacific Writers and Translators (APWT), Axlepino and Anacbanua.

Her poetry and children's stories have been featured in different anthologies and magazines worldwide.

Links to her works:

panitikan.ph/2018/03/30/caroline-nazareno-gabis

apwriters.org/author/ceri_naz/

www.aveviajera.org/nacionesunidasdelasletras/id1181.html

Carolin 'Ceri' Nazareno-Gabis

Ikigai

What is life these days?
Isolated and quarantined.
Where is life as to the moment
Having no time to repent.
Which way you'll going to take?
When all roads seem so bleak and weary,
What does your heart beat?
When everything seem to fleet
Why will you stay late
Overtime, in hurry of things
You own a life to bear,
How will you create a self-care pledge
When you have stolen all the time
To love and be loved
To care and be cared of.
That you never know,
Selfless vs. selfishness,
There is one thing my heart desires
Seeing everything in place
As we smile heartily together
Living un-imprisoned
From worldly splendour.

Mother Earth

you amplify
the whispers
of graceful spirit,
suddenly creates
harmonious lyrical
touches to my heart...

you penetrate beingness
as you caress all creatures
to live the fullest
because you breathe life,
gifting us
 the wonders of nature.

you are the summit
waving flags of biodiversity,
the greeneries filled canopy of hope
fresh wealth of centuries
grow the seeds you want to harvest
graces for a lifetime.

My Summer Rain

Summers are born many days and nights
Scourging heat, that brought pain and sweat
Drenching, draining mind's well
As it cries numbness.

Where's the cold breeze from the veranda
Where's the roving droplets to the rocking chair
Have you ever touched the mist
As you blow your nose,
And wipe the heavenly dews
From your eyes,
When you miss the rain,
And shared cold shower
When we're still together.

Will you be the same
Story of our last petrichor,
In a summer rain?

Swapna Behera

Swapna Behera

Swapna Behera is a bilingual contemporary poet, author, translator and editor from Odisha, India. She was a teacher from 1984 to 2015. Her stories, poems and articles are widely published in National and International journals, and ezines, and are translated into different national and International languages. She has penned six books. She is the recipient of the Prestigious International Mother Language UGADI AWARD WINNER 2019. She was conferred upon the Prestigious International Poesis Award of Honor at the 2nd Bharat Award for Literature as Jury in 2015, The Enchanting Muse Award in India World Poetree Festival 2017, World Icon of Peace Award in 2017, and the Pentasi B World Fellow Poet in 2017. She is the recipient of the Prolific Poetess Award ,The Life time Achievement Award ,The Best Planner Award ,The Sahitya Shiromani Award, ATAL BIHARI BAJPAYEE Award, ATAL Award 2018 ,Global Literature Guardian Award ,International Life Time Achievement Award and the Master of Creative Impulse Award .She has received the Honoured Poet of India from the Seychelles Government accredited Literary Society Lasher one poem A NIGHT IN THE REFUGEE CAMP is translated into 60 languages .She is the Ambassador of Humanity by Hafrikan Prince Art World Africa 2018 and an official member of World Nation's Writers Union ,Kazakhstan2018. Italy, the National President for India by Hispanomundial Union of Writers (UHE), Peru, the administrator of several poetic groups, and the Cultural Ambassador for India and South Asia of Inner Child Press African is the life member of Odisha Environmental Society.

swapna.behera@gmail.com

all art a propaganda

large figure
simple lines
rich colours
with Aztec influence
stories of workers
miners ,labourers ,farmers
profound effect
frescoes ,cubism
and later post impressionism
unique style of light and shadow
art is such profound universal language
art is weapon
"what I saw is not important
what they used me to see is talent"
mural movements of Diego Rivera
revolutionary union of technical workers,
painters who sing the visions of life
the celebration of Cinco de Mayo
art speaks, assimilates ,
liberates and raises voice
lines and curves
march forward ......

the limited version

limited rice
tears of the mother
unlimited love in the family

limited oxygen
tears of the patient
unlimited bodies on the pyres

limited money
tears of the migrants
unlimited blisters on the highways

limited water in the rivers
tears of the nation
unlimited agendas of the seminars

limited alphabets to express love
tears of passion
unlimited commitments to do or die

limited versions converge
to desolate or isolate
in every time zone
 mingle or jingle
for life is a limited version
but if can live for others ;
we shine
the unlimited you and me ......

the arid layers

within the ceramic bowl
a heart, a red hibiscus
couple of radiant moments
do you remember ;
that green coconut with two straws
please ,pause a while
as I wait for the
dew drops

the leaves are still green
busy in thematic struggle
 each morning I crack the layers
i manage my way
for the lyrical harvests
the lost key is hanging
i can see the palace
each room ,the courtyard
molecules of musing
in the layers of time and space
the ink drops are divine blood
it can convert any
 arid layer to a flower garden
so dear ,just wait
no worries ......

Albert 'Infinite' Carrasco

Albert 'Infinite' Carassco

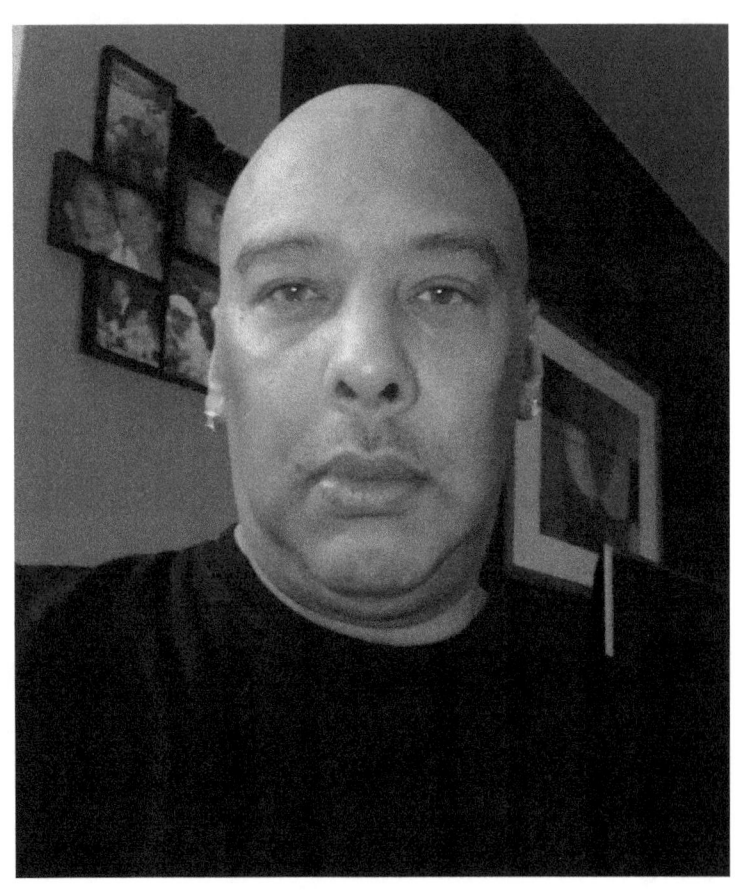

Albert "Infinite The Poet" Carrasco is an urban poet, mentor and public speaker.

Albert believes his experience of growing up in poverty, dealing with drugs and witnessing murder over and over were lessons learnt, in order to gain knowledge to teach. Albert's harsh reality and honesty is a powerfully packed punch delivered through rhyme. Infinite grew up in the east part of the Bronx and still resides there, so he knows many young men will follow the same dark path he followed looking for change. The life of crime should never be an option to being poor but it is, very often.

Infinite poetry @lulu.com

Alcarrasco2 on YouTube

Infinite the poet on reverbnation

Infinite Poetry

http://www.lulu.com/us/en/shop/al-infinite-carrasco/infinite-poetry/paperback/product-21040240.html

Diego Rivera

Diego Rivera was an artist, a Mexican born painter. He saw life in color.
Diego was influenced by post impressionist like Paul Cezanne, Gaugin and Van Gogh.
He came from a middle class family, so he wanted his art to be bought by everyone equally, not just the wealthy.
Mr. rivera traveled abroad and studied the works of those before him,
in Spain, he drew with a cubist stlye for a while,
but that came to an end when he got inspiration to return to his native land to paintings of realism.

Murals became is passion.
He showed the life and times along with the struggle of his people.
Diego Rivera grew up idolizing artist all around the world, in due time, people all over the world admired and idolized him.
From Mexico to Spain and all the way to New York he painted his visions,
the M.O.M.A gave him an opportunity for a one man exhibition.

The antidote

All channels are interrupted by the breaking news world wide... Anchors are ecstatic, some are bawling, happy tears are falling. They did it! they did it! People are celebrating all over, life as we know has changed. Everyone is praising these men and women for their hard work that led to this discovery. We love you!! Thank you!! You're amazing!!. They know, they'll have to answer a lot of questions from television and radio interviews. They're prepared. When will we see the test subjects?... There's a few with us today. How does it work?... If they're still in the hospital, it's a simple injection, if they're at their final destination we'll have to excavate skeletons drill tiny holes in bones, fill them with the medication to regrow flesh until they look exactly as they did before death. When does it go on the market?... Immediately. How much will it cost?... The first time it's free but in order to keep production, anytime after they'll be a fee. Prices will differ depending on families budgets, financing will be available. Do you guys think you can supply the definite demand?... Yes. They'll be factories throughout the continents that will be open twenty four hours a day to produce and store the death reversal antidote.

Ghetto kids

Nights were blue the days were dark,
from dusk till dawn I was the ghetto teen in the park,
I was at rock bottom, so I sold rock to get out of rock bottoms problems,

Our rent was 250, we could never pay on time, So we copped 250's, quarter keys Gathered up all the young brave hearts, And did hand to hand of cooked grams like a mime, we climbed the charts,

Blam blam blam blam blam, eddie ralphy edgar orlando bunca, those five shots five names represent a small portion of the dead brave hearts of mine,

Us ghetto kids were bought up in hells kitchen, A picture, a few candles, we mourned in front of make shift murals, while we continued pitching 5 or 10 dollar fixings, The same reason, why their in six foot ditches, staring up at the eternal ceiling, Us ghetto kids were deemed expendable, organ donors, future vegetables for what went on in our housing vestibule.

Eliza Segiet

Eliza Segiet: Master's Degree in Philosophy, completed postgraduate studies in Cultural Knowledge, Philosophy, Arts and Literature at Jagiellonian University. She is a member of The Association of Polish Writers and The NWNU - Union of Writers of the World.

Her poems *Questions* and *Sea of Mists* won the title of the International Publication of the Year 2017 and 2018 in Spillwords Press.

For her volume of *Magnetic People* she won a literary award of a *Golden Rose* named after Jaroslaw Zielinski (Poland 2019 r.). Her poem The *Sea of Mists* was chosen as one of the best one hundred poems of 2018 by International Poetry Press Publication Canada.

In Poet's Yearbook, as the author of *Sea of Mists*, she was awarded with the prestigious Elite Writer's Status Award as one of the best poets of 2019 (July 2019).

She was awarded *World Poetic Star Award* by World Nations Writers Union – the world's largest Writers' Union from Kazakhstan (August 2019).

In September 2019 she was 1st Place Laureate (Foreign Poetry category) – in Contest *Quando È la Vita ad Invitare* for poem *Be Yourself* (Italy).

Her poem *Order* from volume *Unpaired* was selected as one of the 100 best poems of 2019 in International Poetry Press Publications (Canada).

Nominated for the Pushcart Prize 2019.

Nominated for the iWoman Global Awards (2019).

Laureate Naji Naaman Literary Prize 2020.

Laureate International Award PARAGON OF HOPE (Canada, 2020).

Obtained certificate of appreciation from *Gujarat Sahitya Academy* and *Motivational Strips* for literary excellence par with global standards (2020).

Ambassador of Literature granted by *Motivational Strips*.

Author's works can be found in anthologies, separate books and literary magazines worldwide.

The essence
In the memory of Diego Rivera

Mexican La Cantina
it's not soaked with just the will,
for memory to smolder.
To survive
after getting to the other side
– that's the aim.
The essence of existence is time
to live after living
– the fire of survival.

Translated Ula de B.

Piercing

Among people, pierce
unrecognizable shadows,
but sometime in the light
they will cease to be just them.
It may turn out
that we are
part of the resurrected world.

Mourned long ago
are among us.

Translated by Artur Komoter

Involuntarily

When we are
anointed with life,
marked by destiny,
we wonder
why
the same Demiurge
gives us life and death?
Why
do we have to
agree on destiny?

Often –
involuntarily.

Translated by Artur Komoter

William S. Peters Sr.

William S. Peters, Sr.

Bill's writing career spans a period of over 50 years. Being first Published in 1972, Bill has since went on to Author in excess of 50 additional Volumes of Poetry, Short Stories, etc., expressing his thoughts on matters of the Heart, Spirit, Consciousness and Humanity. His primary focus is that of Love, Peace and Understanding!

Bill says . . .

I have always likened Life to that of a Garden. So, for me, Life is simply about the Seeds we Sow and Nourish. All things we "Think and Do", will "Be" Cause and eventually manifest itself to being an "Effect" within our own personal "Existences" and "Experiences" . . . whether it be Fruit, Flowers, Weeds or Barren Landscapes! Bill highly regards the Fruits of his Labor and wishes that everyone would thus go on to plant "Lovely" Seeds on "Good Ground" in their own Gardens of Life!

to connect with Bill, he is all things Inner Child

www.iaminnerchild.com

Personal Web Site

www.iamjustbill.com

Diego

Diego María de la Concepción Juan Nepomuceno
Estanislao de la Rivera y Barrientos Acosta y Rodríguez

They had more names for me,
But I would rather not repeat them.

My non Frisco Frescos
Started a movement
That disturbed many

I fathered many . . .
Within the art
And without . . .
It was all life for me . . .

I was one
Who just needed
To try different embraces,
Even in the women I loved

Frida was the most notable
And we exploded
Until the day she died . . .
Our volcanic partnership in
Love and art
Spawned yet
Another turning
Of history's page

Read about me

My name is Diego . . .
Diego María de la Concepción Juan Nepomuceno
Estanislao de la Rivera y Barrientos Acosta y Rodríguez

The Plantation Blues

I dun caught me a case
Of those Plantation Blues

You see,
Every once in a while
We Colored Folks,
Or as I like to put it ...
Hued-Mans
Wake Up,
I swear we still
On the Plantation
Yas suh...

We still being hunted,
Killed,
And sometimes hung,
But if you ain't dead yet,
Know that many
Of dem dere other folks
Wish you were!

75 years ago
I be waking up
As a Negro,
Then we was Colored Folk,
Some still called us Niggers
…..
But now ...
I am Black,
I am an African American....
Some times,
Even I has troubles

William S. Peters, Sr.

Understanding who I am,
Especially in the eyes
Of dem otha folks . . .
And sum of dem
Still call us Niggahs

I aintz pickin'
Yo cotton no-mo . .
Maybe that's why youz mad
At me,
At us,
At yo-self.

Seems to me,
We ain't neva gonna be free.
Shit, FREE is just a word they sold
To us.
Told to us
That we could begin to think
We wuz ....
.....
Just ask all dem dere
Brothas and Sistahs
Behind the barbed wire
Adorned in orange jumpsuits ....
Iz dey free? . . .
Have dey ever been?

Yeah, we free to die,
Free to entertain,
Doin' the 'Step and Fetchit' 2 step,
Coonin' our way thru
The BB . . . Bias Bullshit . . .
Yeah, we be free.
Free to shut-up, keep quiet
And remain subservient

I even saw a couple of the ignorant ones
Suggesting ...
Slavery should be brought back ...
Well, I may not be free
In many ways,
But I ain't neva gonna be put
In nobody's chains,
Especially doze mental ones

I am so damn tired of
Being lied on,
Demonized,
Dehumanized,
Deceived,
Exploited,
And used
For target practice

Yeah I think I be comin' down
With a case of
Dem dere Plantation Blues,

If dis is this a dream,
Should I wake up,
If I do,
It def'nly will become
Someone else's nightmare

The Plantation Blues

Moving on . . .

He walked hungrily.
Through the fields
Seeking . . .
Seeking what,
He did not know . . .
In particular,
He just knew
That it existed . . .
Something
That was calling loudly
To his soul

He walked hungrily.
Through the fields

And some times he ran

Moving On . . .

May 2021 Featured Poets

~ * ~

Paramita Mukherjee Mullick

Jaydeep Sarangi

Rose Zerguine

Bismay Mohanty

Paramita Mukherjee Mullick

Paramita Mukherjee Mullick

Dr. Paramita Mukherjee Mullick is a scientist transformed into a well-loved poet. She has six books and her poems have been widely published in India and abroad. A few of her poems have been translated into 39 languages. Paramita has been blessed with numerous awards like the Nobel Laureate Rabindranath Tagore award, Poetess of Elegance 2019 award and many more. She started and is the President of the Mumbai Chapter of the Intercultural Poetry and Performance Library where she promotes fusion of poetry with other performing arts. She also promotes indigenous poetry, peace poetry and multilingual poetry. She received the Gold Rose from MS Productions, Buenos Aires for promoting literature and culture. She is an editor as well, edited an international journal previously and is editing for a publishing house at present. She lives in Mumbai, India with her husband and daughter.

The Search for Completeness

The new mother looks at the smile of her child.
Her heart fills with joy.
The new human fills her heart.
A happiness more than any jazzy toy.

A mother and wife, looks after her family.
Feeds them and lovingly them nourish.
Selfless, compassionate and kind.
Her happiness to see her children and husband flourish.

A father and a husband, toils the whole day.
To make the family prosperous and comfortable.
Only others in his mind when working hard.
Bringing his family members in the forefront and making them able.

The giving of oneself to another.
An emotion which is all above.
The search for completeness ends with this emotion.
It is the definition less, fathomless love.

Impermanence

The yellow leaves on the branch became yellow and fell off.
Green new leaves sprouted on the branch again.
A brief shower of rain quenched the thirst of the earth.
The sweet-smelling earth heaved a sigh of relief.
The kingfisher fleeted by, here it was and then lost from sight.
Its dazzling colours lingering in my eyes.
Suddenly the melodious music from the flute player on the street.
Arouses my senses and I get immersed in that music.
Such is the magic of impermanence.
The short spell enchants us.
A brief encounter with a stranger,
May lead to a beautiful friendship.
These moments are to be cherished and preserved.
Time for such beautiful moments to be reserved.

From Darkness to Light

From darkness to light
I walk on and on.
The road clears in front of me.
I open my eyes and YOU I see.

From ignorance to knowledge
I walk on and on.
The knots open, the path clears.
YOU make me walk with my dears.

From hatred to forgiveness
I walk on and on.
Sadness gives way to happiness in the journey.
I look inside and see YOU in me.

Jaydeep Sarangi

Jaydeep Sarangi

Jaydeep Sarangi is a widely anthologized and reviewed bilingual poet with eight collections in English latest being *Heart Raining the Light (2020)*released in Rome. Sarangi has read his poems in different shores of the globe. His later readings were at Flinders University, University of Western Australia, University of South Australia,University of Wollongong, Perth Poetry Club(Australia), University of Udine(Italy)and University of Rezeszow(Poland). Sarangi is on the editorial boards of different journals featuring poetry and articles on poetry like *Mascara Literary Review*, *Transnational Literature*, (Australia), *Teesta*, *WEC*(India) . Among his recent awards, the Setu Award of Excellence for 2019(Petersburg, USA).He is a professor of English and principal at New Alipore College, Kolkata.. E mail: jaydeepsarangi@gmail.com

Jaydeep Sarangi

Social Distancing

a spam
a troll
swear words flare up.
My bones are
sleeping in a tent,
selfie embracing ideas.
Life is just flaming
here, and beyond.
beyond contacts,
Fast fading and sharing
The face is no face.
Mobile screen is a romantic halo.
The Moon makes no one lunatic.

All virtual. All for a passing stint.

.

Happy Days

A blue lid, frayed at its edges,
used excessively, day and night.
It only yearns for what it has lost
in the company of distance and days.

Let us press hard, and all shall see
Glory of our happy Deity.
After this spell of rain.

Jaydeep Sarangi

My Sweet Home Town

There is peace after a homely noise
my mother sleeps safe after the evening chants.

The earth watches
I take the pigeons out every day.

Every pain has a remedy
with men and women rising.

Fair green Mistress
I bear a rooted grief.

I speak with your words.
I peel out juice of happiness.

Rose Zerguine

Rose Zerguine

WARDA ZERGUINE Is born in Guelma (east of ALGERIA)

She is a writer, researcher in the popular oral tradition and Journalist (member of union algerian journalists), also she was a former senior executive in "ALGERIENNE DES EAUX". WARDA ZERGUINE has published 03 works, a book entitled : "ALANKOUD" on folk proverbs and popular puzzles, "IllUMINATIONS" about the revolutionary folk songs in Guelma region and "JAWAHAR" a second part of the folk proverbs and popular puzzles.

She Participated in many festivals in algeria – tunisia – jordan .

And participated in different international anthologies : mesopotamia cultural center belgrade –serbia- on 2018 , 2019 and 2020 , collection of universal poetry "jasmine and love collars" in tunisia.

She wrote and recited different poems in different languages : arrabic , english and french.
She is a member of algerian artists.

Rose Zerguine

Love at the time of the siege

At the crossroads of climb
Be my lover
O wave that carried me
Tide is no longer scary
And no longer in the doll fountain
Except your love
Pull me chest swing to you
From you picked up my wedding
I flirt with staying
O you who drowned me
Do you wipe off my maps?
Or pick me up from exile gazelle
For my seasons I love you
he said to equal text
Its depreciable text
I love you he said
Do not migrate except to my blood
You are my mirror to see me
I comb your pillow and sleep
Almighty says that I do not stay alone
I fear my estrangement from me
You be my compass to reach you
My love, you are the Transfiguration
If I have a love disk in my left
My love, you are a Lust for the character
If I have the texts of love with my right
I love you to be the beginning
And I love you to be the end

DECISION

I'm not from you
You are not from me
You are not of my bread and my provision
You are not a specter of my nostalgia
You are not an extension creek
You're not the crazy melody
You are not a glimmer of my heart
You are not the whisper of my eyelids
And you are not the flow of observer
I'm looking at you .. Maybe
And maybe..
My call is calling me
My country is not your country
And my sky is not your sky
My refusal is a spiritual mystery
And beyond your imagination
And my ambition ..
From my passion
Explodes stubborn rock
So build ..
Ruin
What is impossible to build
You are not mine
When you said
Let's go ..
We manage
Our high star
Let him draw our path
Give him gifts
Maybe he is satisfied
I'm not from you
When you call ..

Rose Zerguine

In humility and supplication
Keep an eye on delayed bereavement
And honorable dignities
Hey..
Hold on
The will of the universe
Is an action ..
Determination
Refusal..
And heaven's decision
You who are not of me..
Do not say..
Luck wants.

Tales

They told me in my boyhood..
About a lot..
About evil spirits
ghosts..
and Goblins..
I became the one who loved the stories..
a long time ago..
I take every opportunity
I race time to know..
What I don't know..
But I know
That my fear
From the praises of the story..
And here we grow
And These stories never grew
On my growing fear..
a long time ago..
We are not from Him
Yesterday we wanted fear..
We did not hide
From the stories of robbery
And then we became like those stories.
And any stories..?
We have turned to everything
How to share bread
And a cup of milk
The important..
The ceiling of the tale brings us together
And boy's hymns..
The important..
Everything is shared..
The joy of the little child

Rose Zerguine

Painful heart pain
Everything is shared
We fear for our stories..
And our ogres..
Goblins
a long time ago..
all beautiful turned down
toughing we would build beautifully..
So we woke up on stories..
There are no trust goblins..
And no ghosts
The bread is no longer a melody..
Even if it is not shared
I don't know my way
I may be from not.

Bismay Mohanty

Bismay Mohanty

Bismay is an IT professional from India who is currently also pursuing a degree in English. He has published two poetry books till now and is working on his short story collection. He loves cycling, have bibliophile friends and plays PC games in his spare time. Having a keen interest in literature, he also helps his juniors achieve their writing potentials by guiding with whatever available resources.

He first got published in YOTP back in January 2015 when he was in high school. After finishing his degree, he now aims to make the best use of his skills and is under constant learning for the same. Naturally, Bismay feels 'The Power of the Subconscious Mind' by Joseph Murphy as his guardian angel book, which he believes to have miraculously brought many improvisations to his way of writing.

You can reach out to him at bismaymohantypoetry@gmail.com

Bismay Mohanty

A decade ago

Not long back, one day
She stood at the balcony.
Her brother's friend had come to meet him
The boy on cycle looked at her blank
As if never seen a girl before
Or never someone so beautiful
Did she match his imagination?
Of fictional characters
In books and movies.

She smiled at him
And kept smiling back each time
When she knew that he came daily
Just to see her in the evening
From the same balcony-road distance
Properly maintained;
No, the era wasn't that of the pandemic
When people stood at distance
And wore masks,
Love was always a virus though.

She recalls today on the same balcony
When the friends are no more there
Who claimed 'You deserve better!'
Seeing his curly hair and skeletal body,
And various aspects that were not proper.
He no longer comes to see her
After standing there for hours
Through winters and all summer,
Heavy rain not to forget at all;
She never made any effort.

In the twenty first century,
When parents disown children
If they aren't born as intended,

He denies to learn it right away
That stories in real don't resemble
Those they show in books and movies,
Who will want to relate to a tragedy?
Even when the same exists and we all live it
It would have been different, if decades ago
Had society taken AK Ramanujan seriously.

A few decades later again
Now he wanders lonely as a ghost,
She stands still at the balcony for hours,
Kin of either family are now long gone,
Now they both think in their despondency
If all their lives were a life, trying to figure
Why do we glorify hatred with bullets and bomb?
And find love all the more explicit
Nevertheless, his funeral passed the same road
Where her grey hair flew and landed on him.

Friends of formalities

Hello you Sir!
That you are cutting off calls
For you don't want to quaver
Rather show not to anyone
That times can be tougher
Why care for it an image after all?
Oh! Are you a motivational speaker?
Doesn't matter any if you hide anyway
Sure, let distress give you tremor
Cry, sleep, lose appetite, love insomnia
This schedule can go on forever
Otherwise, you could talk you know?
But with whom? That question is a fever
Try and trust once, not again will you
When the interest or ability to solve is mere
Still let's be in touch, after all you can die
Without my "Happy Birthday Dear"!

Turn Around

Left the music player back at home
Today I wanted to listen to myself
Showed myself the moon at its brightest white
There is much beauty in the endless streetlights
Extending their ways up to infinity
Honking buses have tired passengers returning home
Excited children on bikes and cars in opposite direction
Such visual along with the pleasant air that flew
A scooter passes by and I gaze
A girl as she turns around
To look me in the eye
And recall hauntings of the past
With all love and prayers to Almighty
No sooner did the pleasant atmosphere go
And became the nature a dark realm of ghosts
Shrieking about the nights where there were cries
Ruminating upon an idea of the value
Of people who do not remain at hard times
Let feelings pass like the bad old days
Time would come and both will eventually forget
The mere existence of each other
And it was all fine till this evening
Hallucinating one epitaphs on the sidewalk
Adoring "dead in love" over it
Withdrawing from the great idea
I turned back to walk my way home.

Bismay Mohanty

Remembering

our fallen soldiers of verse

Janet Perkins Caldwell
February 14, 1959 ~ September 20, 2016

Alan W. Jankowski
16 March 1961 ~ 10 March 2017

Now available

World Healing World Peace
2020

Poets for Humanity

Inner Child Press News

Poetry Posse Members

We are so excited to share and announce a few of the current books, as well as the new and upcoming books of some of our Poetry Posse authors.

On the following pages we present to you ...

Jackie Davis Allen

Gail Weston Shazor

hülya n. yılmaz

Nizar Sartawi

Faleeha Hassan

Fahredin Shehu

Caroline 'Ceri' Nazareno

Eliza Segiet

Teresa E. Gallion

William S. Peters, Sr.

The Year of the Poet VIII ~ May 2021

Now Available
www.innerchildpress.com

Inner Child Press News

Now Available
www.innerchildpress.com

The Year of the Poet VIII ~ May 2021

Now Available
www.innerchildpress.com

Inner Child Press News

Now Available at
www.amazon.com/gp/product/B08MYL5B7S/ref=dbs_a_def_rwt_hsch_vapi_tkin_p1_i2

The Year of the Poet VIII ~ May 2021

Now Available at
www.innerchildpress.com

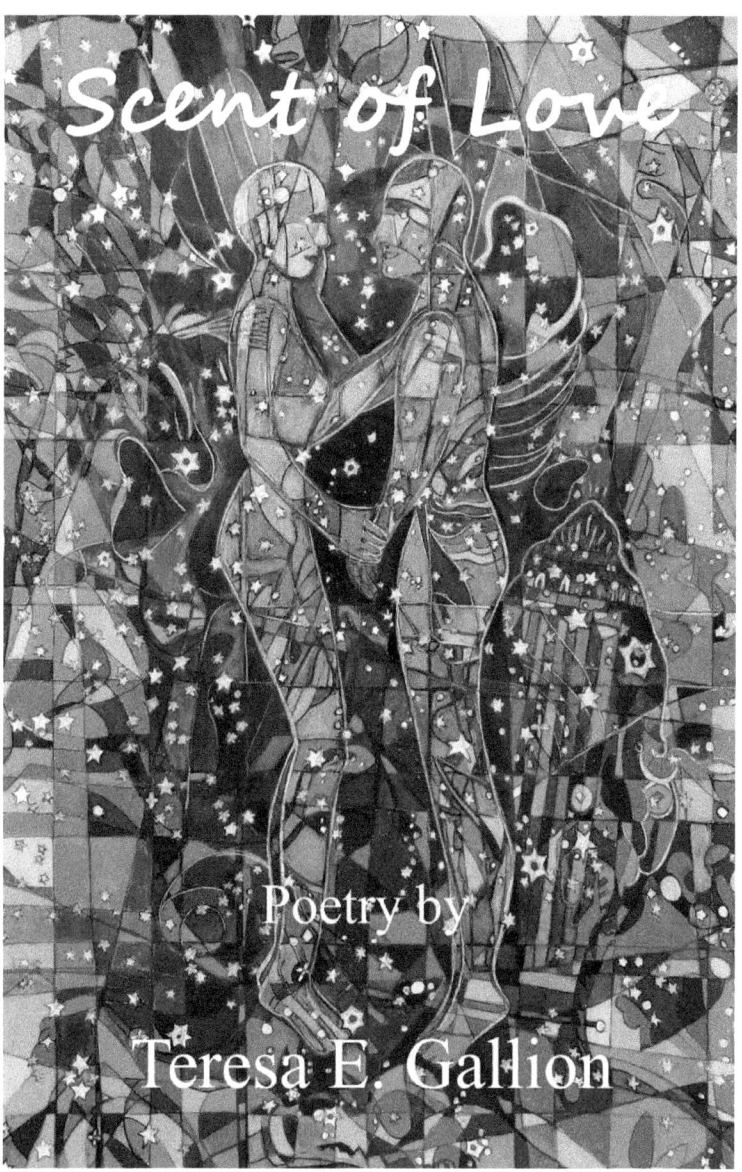

Scent of Love

Poetry by

Teresa E. Gallion

Inner Child Press News

Now Available
www.innerchildpress.com

Now Available
www.innerchildpress.com

Inner Child Press News

Now Available
www.innerchildpress.com

COMING SOON
www.innerchildpress.com

The Book of krisar

volume v

william s. peters, sr.

Inner Child Press News

Now Available
www.innerchildpress.com

The Book of krisar

Volume I

william s. peters, sr.

The Book of krisar

Volume II

william s. peters, sr.

Now Available
www.innerchildpress.com

The Book of krisar
Volume III

william s. peters, sr.

The Book of krisar
Volume IV

william s. peters, sr.

Inner Child Press News

Now Available
www.innerchildpress.com

The Year of the Poet VIII ~ May 2021

Now Available
www.innerchildpress.com

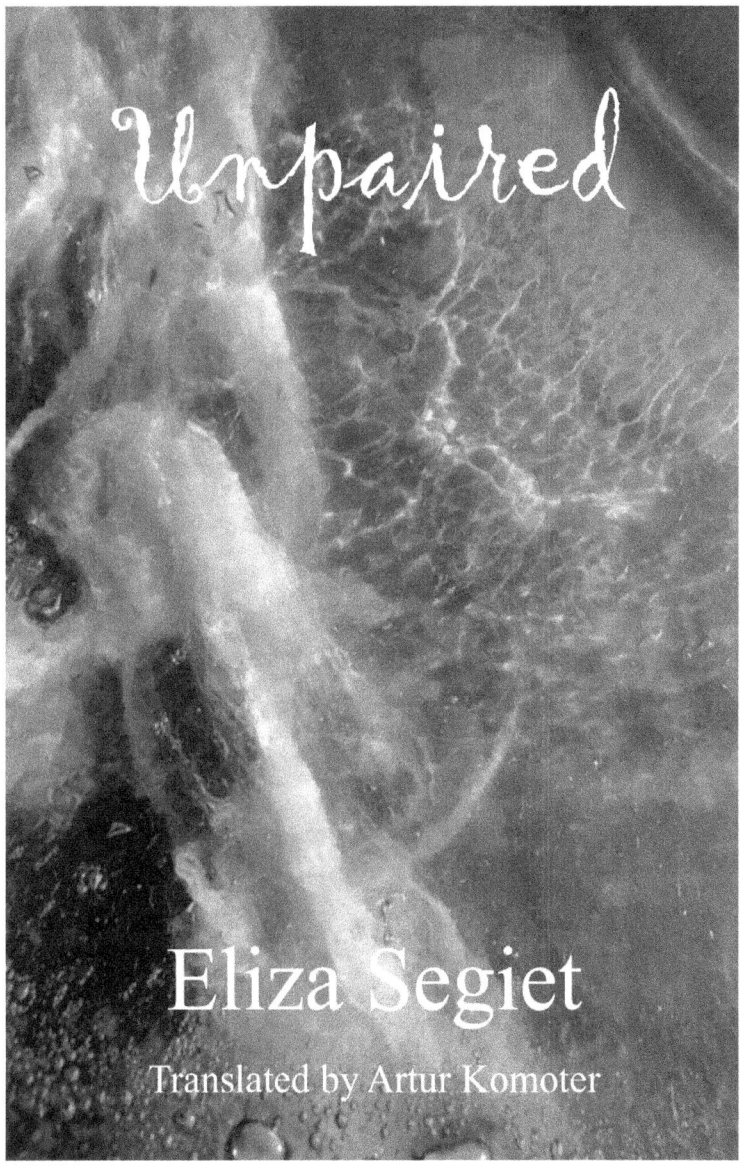

Inner Child Press News

Private Issue
www.innerchildpress.com

The Year of the Poet VIII ~ May 2021

Now Available
www.innerchildpress.com

Inner Child Press News

Now Available at
www.innerchildpress.com

The Year of the Poet VIII ~ May 2021

Now Available at
www.innerchildpress.com

Inner Child Press News

Now Available at
www.innerchildpress.com

Now Available at
www.innerchildpress.com

HERENOW

FAHREDIN SHEHU

Inner Child Press News

Now Available at
www.innerchildpress.com

Now Available at
www.innerchildpress.com

Inner Child Press News

Now Available at
www.innerchildpress.com

The Year of the Poet VIII ~ May 2021

Now Available at
www.innerchildpress.com

Inner Child Press News

Now Available at
www.innerchildpress.com

The Year of the Poet VIII ~ May 2021

Now Available at
www.innerchildpress.com

Breakfast

for

Butterflies

Faleeha Hassan

Inner Child Press News

Now Available at
www.innerchildpress.com

The Year of the Poet VIII ~ May 2021

Now Available at
www.innerchildpress.com

inner child press
presents

Tunisia My Love

william s. peters, sr.

Inner Child Press News

Now Available at
www.innerchildpress.com

The Year of the Poet VIII ~ May 2021

Now Available at
www.innerchildpress.com

william s. peters, sr.

Other

Anthological

works from

Inner Child Press International

www.innerchildpress.com

Inner Child Press Anthologies

World Healing World Peace 2020

Poets for Humanity

Now Available
www.worldhealingworldpeacepoetry.com

Inner Child Press Anthologies

Now Available
www.innerchildpress.com

Inner Child Press Anthologies

Inner Child Press International
&
The Year of the Poet
present

Poetry
the best of 2020

Poets of the World

Now Available
www.innerchildpress.com

Inner Child Press Anthologies

Now Available
www.innerchildpress.com

Inner Child Press Anthologies

the Heart of a Poet

words for a better tomorrow

The Conscious Poets

Now Available
www.innerchildpress.com

Inner Child Press Anthologies

Now Available
www.innerchildpress.com

Inner Child Press Anthologies

Now Available at
www.innerchildpress.com

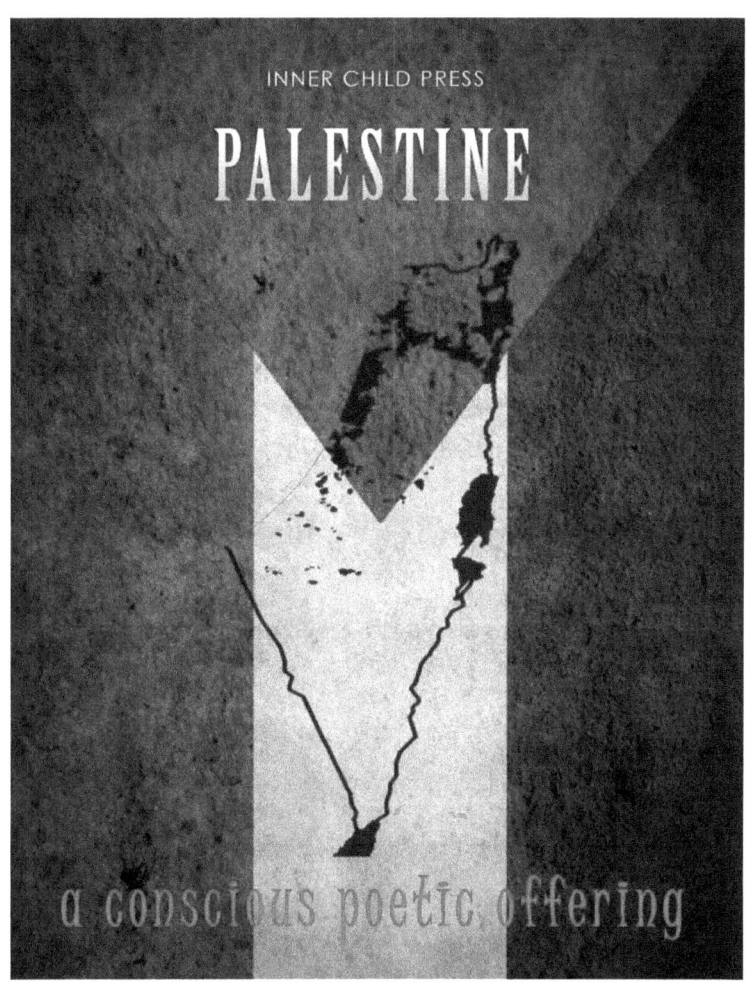

Now Available at
www.innerchildpress.com

Inner Child Press Anthologies

Now Available at
www.innerchildpress.com

Inner Child Press Anthologies

Inner Child Press International
presents

A Love Anthology
2019

The Love Poets

Now Available

www.worldhealingworldpeacepoetry.com

Inner Child Press Anthologies

Now Available

www.worldhealingworldpeacepoetry.com

Inner Child Press Anthologies

Now Available

www.worldhealingworldpeacepoetry.com

Inner Child Press Anthologies

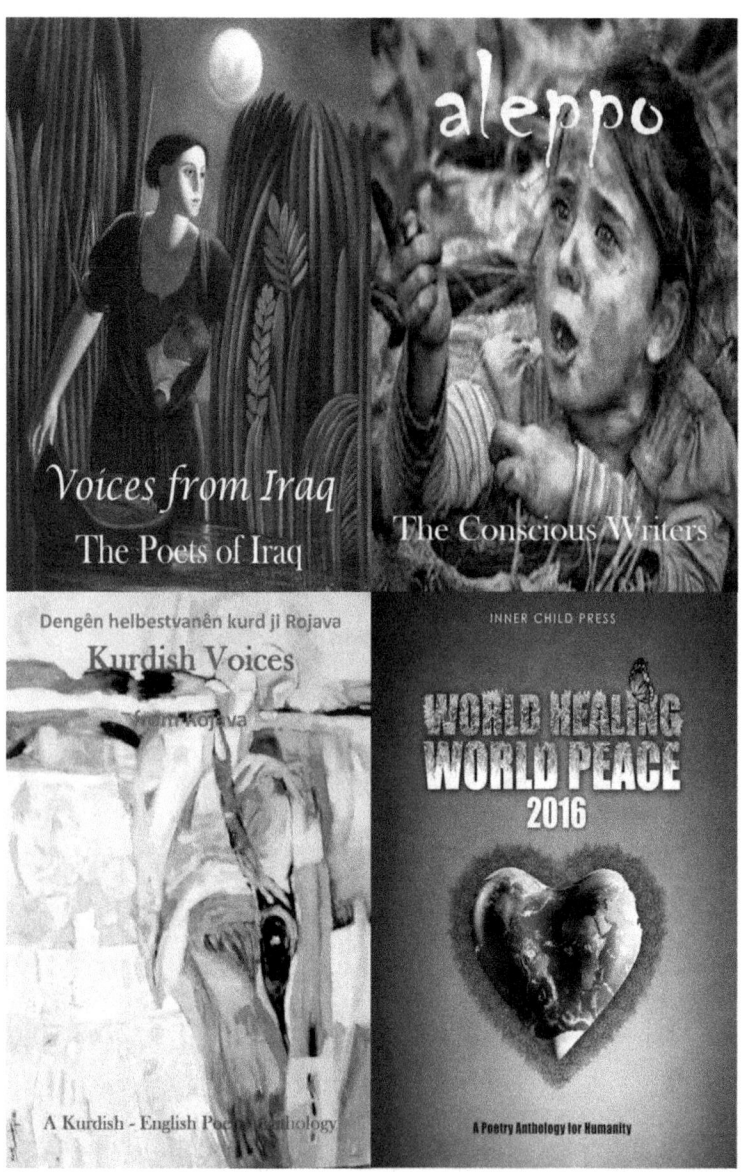

Now Available

www.innerchildpress.com/anthologies

Inner Child Press Anthologies

Now Available

www.innerchildpress.com/anthologies

Inner Child Press Anthologies

Now Available

www.innerchildpress.com/anthologies

Inner Child Press Anthologies

Now Available

www.innerchildpress.com/anthologies

Inner Child Press Anthologies

Now Available

www.innerchildpress.com/anthologies

Inner Child Press Anthologies

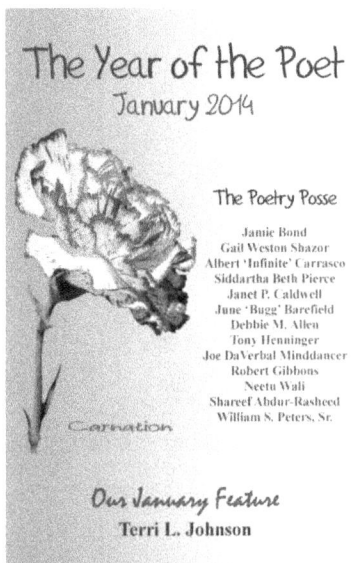

Now Available

www.innerchildpress.com/the-year-of-the-poet

Inner Child Press Anthologies

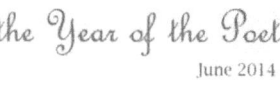

Now Available

www.innerchildpress.com/the-year-of-the-poet

Inner Child Press Anthologies

Now Available

www.innerchildpress.com/the-year-of-the-poet

Inner Child Press Anthologies

Now Available

www.innerchildpress.com/the-year-of-the-poet

Inner Child Press Anthologies

The Year of the Poet II
May 2015

May's Featured Poets
Geri Algeri
Akin Mosi Chinnery
Anna Jakubczak

Emeralds

The Poetry Posse 2015
Jamie Bond * Gail Weston Shazor * Albert 'Infinite' Carrasco
Siddartha Beth Pierce * Janet P. Caldwell * Tony Henninger
Joe DaVerbal Minddancer * Neetu Wali * Shareef Abdur-Rasheed
Kimberly Burnham * Ann White * Keith Alan Hamilton
Katherine Wyatt * Fahredin Shehu * Hülya N. Yılmaz
Teresa E. Gallion * Jackie Allen * William S. Peters, Sr.

The Year of the Poet II
June 2015

June's Featured Poets
Xxxxx xxxxxxxx * xxxxx xx xxxxx * xxxxxx x xxxxx

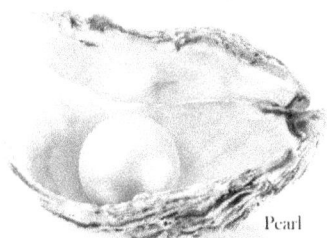

Pearl

The Poetry Posse 2015
Jamie Bond * Gail Weston Shazor * Albert 'Infinite' Carrasco
Siddartha Beth Pierce * Janet P. Caldwell * Tony Henninger
Joe DaVerbal Minddancer * Neetu Wali * Shareef Abdur-Rasheed
Kimberly Burnham * Ann White * Keith Alan Hamilton
Katherine Wyatt * Fahredin Shehu * Hülya N. Yılmaz
Teresa E. Gallion * Jackie Allen * William S. Peters, Sr.

The Year of the Poet II
July 2015

The Featured Poets for July 2015
Abhik Shome * Christina Neal * Robert Neal

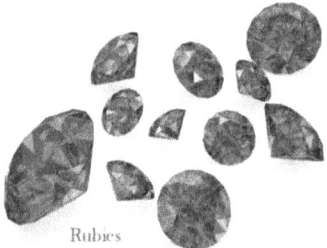

Rubies

The Poetry Posse 2015
Jamie Bond * Gail Weston Shazor * Albert 'Infinite' Carrasco
Siddartha Beth Pierce * Janet P. Caldwell * Tony Henninger
Joe DaVerbal Minddancer * Neetu Wali * Shareef Abdur-Rasheed
Kimberly Burnham * Ann White * Keith Alan Hamilton
Katherine Wyatt * Fahredin Shehu * Hülya N. Yılmaz
Teresa E. Gallion * Jackie Allen * William S. Peters, Sr.

The Year of the Poet II
August 2015

Peridot

Featured Poets
Gayle Howell
Ann Chalasz
Christopher Schultz

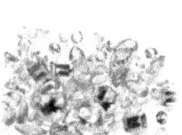

The Poetry Posse 2015
Jamie Bond * Gail Weston Shazor * Albert 'Infinite' Carrasco
Siddartha Beth Pierce * Janet P. Caldwell * Tony Henninger
Joe DaVerbal Minddancer * Neetu Wali * Shareef Abdur-Rasheed
Kimberly Burnham * Ann White * Keith Alan Hamilton
Katherine Wyatt * Fahredin Shehu * Hülya N. Yılmaz
Teresa E. Gallion * Jackie Allen * William S. Peters, Sr.

Now Available

www.innerchildpress.com/the-year-of-the-poet

Inner Child Press Anthologies

Now Available

www.innerchildpress.com/the-year-of-the-poet

Now Available

www.innerchildpress.com/the-year-of-the-poet

Inner Child Press Anthologies

Now Available

www.innerchildpress.com/the-year-of-the-poet

Now Available

www.innerchildpress.com/the-year-of-the-poet

Inner Child Press Anthologies

Now Available

www.innerchildpress.com/the-year-of-the-poet

Inner Child Press Anthologies

Now Available

www.innerchildpress.com/the-year-of-the-poet

Inner Child Press Anthologies

The Year of the Poet IV
September 2017

Featured Poets
Martina Reisz Newberry
Ameer Nassir
Christine Fulco Neal
Robert Neal

The Elm Tree

The Poetry Posse 2017

Gail Weston Shazor * Caroline Nazareno * Bismay Mohanty
Teresa E. Gallion * Anna Jakubczak Vel Ratty Adalan
Joe DaVerbal Minddancer * Shareef Abdur – Rasheed
Albert Carrasco * Kimberly Burnham * Elizabeth Castillo
Hülya N. Yılmaz * Faleeha Hassan * Jackie Davis Allen
Jen Walls * Nizar Sartawi * * William S. Peters, Sr.

The Year of the Poet IV
October 2017

Featured Poets
Ahmed Abu Saleem
Nedal Al-Qaeim
Sadeddin Shahin

The Black Walnut Tree

The Poetry Posse 2017

Gail Weston Shazor * Caroline Nazareno * Bismay Mohanty
Teresa E. Gallion * Anna Jakubczak Vel Ratty Adalan
Joe DaVerbal Minddancer * Shareef Abdur – Rasheed
Albert Carrasco * Kimberly Burnham * Elizabeth Castillo
Hülya N. Yılmaz * Faleeha Hassan * Jackie Davis Allen
Jen Walls * Nizar Sartawi * * William S. Peters, Sr.

The Year of the Poet IV
November 2017

Featured Poets
Kay Peters
Alfreda D. Ghee
Gabriella Garofalo
Rosemary Cappello

The Tree of Life

The Poetry Posse 2017

Gail Weston Shazor * Caroline Nazareno * Bismay Mohanty
Teresa E. Gallion * Anna Jakubczak Vel Ratty Adalan
Joe DaVerbal Minddancer * Shareef Abdur – Rasheed
Albert Carrasco * Kimberly Burnham * Elizabeth Castillo
Hülya N. Yılmaz * Faleeha Hassan * Jackie Davis Allen
Jen Walls * Nizar Sartawi * William S. Peters, Sr.

The Year of the Poet IV
December 2017

Featured Poets
Justice Clarke
Mariel M. Pabroa
Kiley Brown

The Fig Tree

The Poetry Posse 2017

Gail Weston Shazor * Caroline Nazareno * Bismay Mohanty
Teresa E. Gallion * Anna Jakubczak Vel Ratty Adalan
Joe DaVerbal Minddancer * Shareef Abdur – Rasheed
Albert Carrasco * Kimberly Burnham * Elizabeth Castillo
Hülya N. Yılmaz * Faleeha Hassan * Jackie Davis Allen
Jen Walls * Nizar Sartawi * William S. Peters, Sr.

Now Available

www.innerchildpress.com/the-year-of-the-poet

Inner Child Press Anthologies

The Year of the Poet V
January 2018

Featured Poets
Iyad Shamasnah
Yasmeen Hamzeh
Ali Abdolrezaei

Aksum

The Poetry Posse 2018

Gail Weston Shazor * Caroline Nazareno * Tezmin Ition Tsai
Hülya N. Yılmaz * Faleeha Hassan * Jackie Davis Allen
Teresa E. Gallion * Anna Jakubczak Vel Ratty Adalan
Aliça Maria Kuberska * Shareef Abdur – Rasheed
Kimberly Burnham * Elizabeth Castillo
Nizar Sartawi * William S. Peters, Sr.

The Year of the Poet V
February 2018

Sabean

Featured Poets
Muhammad Azram
Anna Szawracka
Abbilipsa Kuanar
Aanika Aory

The Poetry Posse 2018

Gail Weston Shazor * Caroline Nazareno * Tezmin Ition Tsai
Hülya N. Yılmaz * Faleeha Hassan * Jackie Davis Allen
Teresa E. Gallion * Anna Jakubczak Vel Ratty Adalan
Aliça Maria Kuberska * Shareef Abdur – Rasheed
Kimberly Burnham * Elizabeth Castillo
Nizar Sartawi * William S. Peters, Sr.

The Year of the Poet V
March 2018

Featured Poets
Irum Fatima 'Ashi
Cassandra Swan
Jaleel Khazaal
Shazea Zaman

Caribbean
&
Middle America

The Poetry Posse 2018

Gail Weston Shazor * Nizar Sartawi * Hülya N. Yılmaz
Jackie Davis Allen * Caroline Ceri Nazareno
Aliça Maria Kuberska * Teresa E. Gallion
Faleeha Hassan * Shareef Abdur – Rasheed
Kimberly Burnham * Elizabeth Castillo
Tezmin Ition Tsai * William S. Peters, Sr.

The Year of the Poet V
April 2018

Featured Poets

The Nez Perce

The Poetry Posse 2018

Now Available

www.innerchildpress.com/the-year-of-the-poet

Inner Child Press Anthologies

Now Available

www.innerchildpress.com/the-year-of-the-poet

Inner Child Press Anthologies

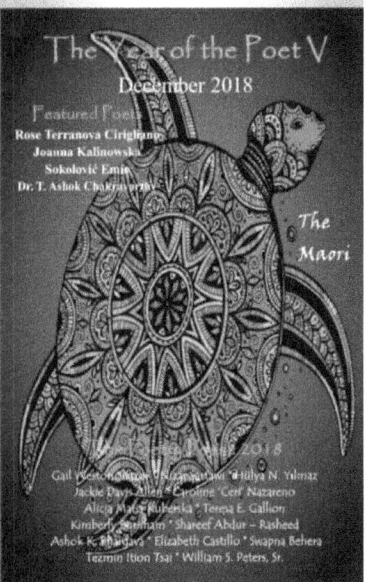

Now Available

www.innerchildpress.com/the-year-of-the-poet

Inner Child Press Anthologies

The Year of the Poet VI
January 2019

Indigenous North Americans

Featured Poets

Houda Elfchtali
Anthony Briscoe
Irani Fatima 'Ashi'
Dr. K. K. Mathew

Dream Catcher

The Poetry Posse 2019

Gail Weston Shazor * Joe Paire * Hülya N. Yılmaz
Jackie Davis Allen * Caroline Nazareno * Eliza Segiet
Alicja Maria Kubenska * Teresa E. Gallion
Kimberly Burnham * Shareef Abdur – Rasheed
Ashok K. Bhargava * Elizabeth Castillo * Swapna Behera
Tezmin Ition Tsai * William S. Peters, Sr.

The Year of the Poet VI
February 2019

Featured Poets

Marek Lukaszewicz * Bharati Nayak
Aida G. Roque * Jean-Jacques Fournier

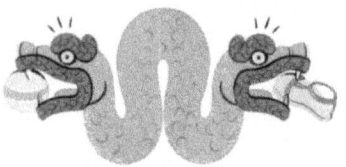

Meso-America

The Poetry Posse 2019

Gail Weston Shazor * Albert Carrasco * Hülya N. Yılmaz
Jackie Davis Allen * Caroline Nazareno * Eliza Segiet
Alicja Maria Kubenska * Teresa E. Gallion * Joe Paire
Kimberly Burnham * Shareef Abdur – Rasheed
Ashok K. Bhargava * Elizabeth Castillo * Swapna Behera
Tezmin Ition Tsai * William S. Peters, Sr.

Now Available

www.innerchildpress.com/the-year-of-the-poet

Inner Child Press Anthologies

Now Available

www.innerchildpress.com/the-year-of-the-poet

Inner Child Press Anthologies

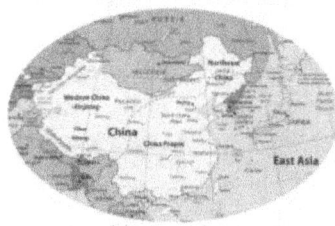

Now Available

www.innerchildpress.com/the-year-of-the-poet

Inner Child Press Anthologies

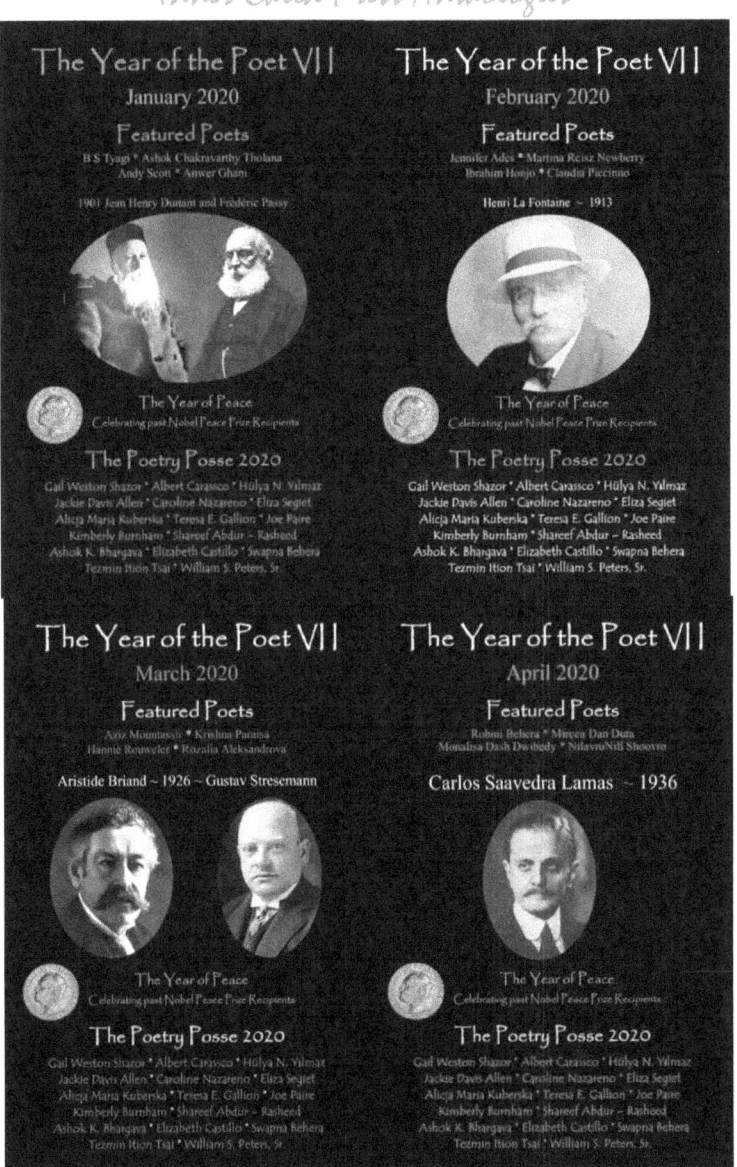

Now Available

www.innerchildpress.com/the-year-of-the-poet

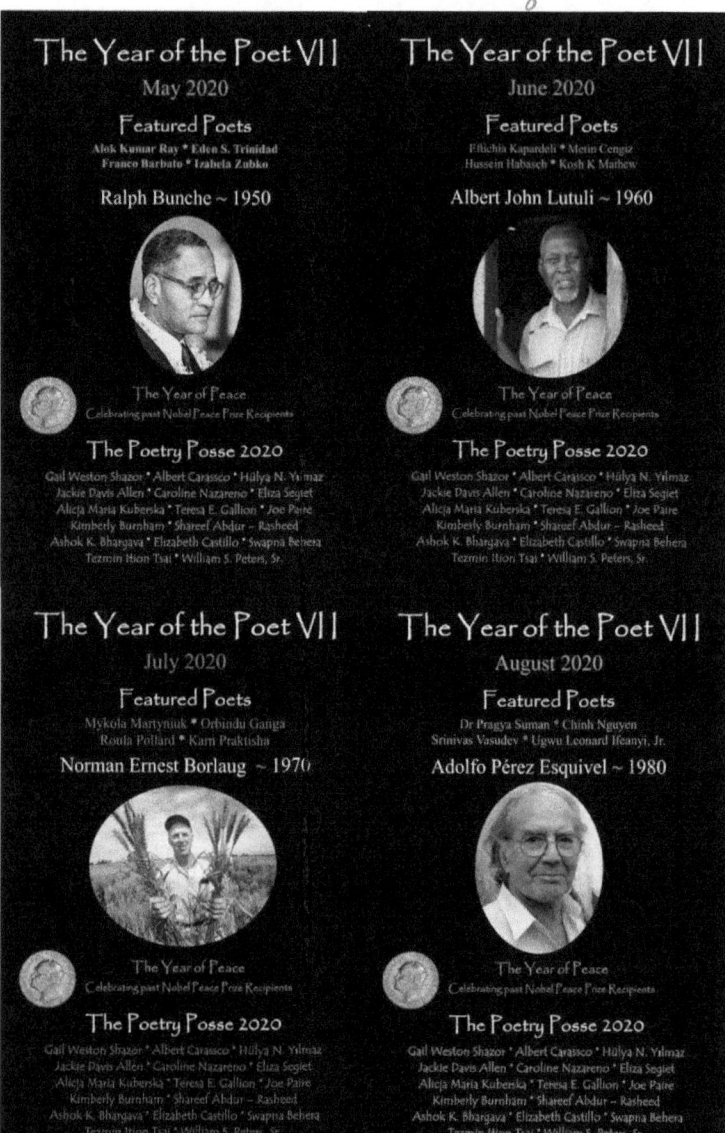

Now Available

www.innerchildpress.com/the-year-of-the-poet

Inner Child Press Anthologies

Now Available

www.innerchildpress.com/the-year-of-the-poet

and there is much, much more !

visit . . .

www.innerchildpress.com/anthologies-sales-special.php

Also check out our Authors and all the wonderful Books Available at :

www.innerchildpress.com/authors-pages

World Healing World Peace 2020

Poets for Humanity

Now Available

www.worldhealingworldpeacepoetry.com

Now Available

www.worldhealingworldpeacepoetry.com

www.worldhealingworldpeacepoetry.com

World Healing World Peace
2012, 2014, 2016, 2018, 2020

Now Available

www.worldhealingworldpeacepoetry.com

Inner Child Press International

'building bridges of cultural understanding'

Meet the Board of Directors

William S. Peters, Sr.
Chair Person
Founder
Inner Child Enterprises
Inner Child Press

Hülya N Yılmaz
Director
Editing Services
Co-Chair Person

Fahredin B. Shehu
Director
Cultural Affairs

Elizabeth E. Castillo
Director
Recording Secretary

De'Andre Hawthorne
Director
Performance Poetry

Gail Weston Shazor
Director
Anthologies

Kimberly Burnham
Director
Cultural Ambassador
Pacific Northwest
USA

Ashok K. Bhargava
Director
WIN Awards

Deborah Smart
Director
Publicity
Marketing

www.innerchildpress.com

Inner Child Press International

'building bridges of cultural understanding'

Meet our Cultural Ambassadors

Fahredin Shehu
Director of Cultural

Faleha Hassan
Iraq – USA

Elizabeth E. Castillo
Philippines

Antoinette Coleman
Chicago
Midwest USA

Ananda Nepali
Nepal – Tibet
Northern India

Kimberly Burnham
Pacific Northwest
USA

Alicja Kuberska
Poland
Eastern Europe

Swapna Behera
India
Southeast Asia

Kolade O. Freedom
Nigeria
West Africa

Monsif Beroual
Morocco
Northern Asia

Ashok K. Bhargava
Canada

Tzemin Ition Tsai
Republic of China
Greater China

Alicia M. Ramirez
Mexico
Central America

Christena AV Williams
Jamaica
Caribbean

Louise Hudon
Eastern Canada

Aziz Mountassir
Morocco
Western Africa

Shareef Abdur-Rasheed
Southeastern USA

Laure Charazac
France
Western Europe

Mohammad Ikbal Harb
Lebanon
Middle East

Mohamed Abdel
Aziz Shmels
Egypt
Middle East

Hilary Mainga
Kenya
Eastern Africa

Josephus R. Johnson
Liberia

www.innerchildpress.com

This Anthological Publication
is underwritten solely by

Inner Child Press International

Inner Child Press is a Publishing Company Founded and Operated by Writers. Our personal publishing experiences provides us an intimate understanding of the sometimes daunting challenges Writers, New and Seasoned may face in the Business of Publishing and Marketing their Creative "Written Work".

For more Information

Inner Child Press International

www.innerchildpress.com

'building bridges of cultural understanding'
202 Wiltree Court, State College, Pennsylvania 16801
www.innerchildpress.com

~ fini ~

www.ingramcontent.com/pod-product-compliance
Lightning Source LLC
LaVergne TN
LVHW051047080426
835508LV00019B/1740